Author's Words

Greetings,

Poetry Corner is a collection of short poems I wrote to encourage myself in the faith. I hope you are inspired by them.

Zikomo Ambuye*
Meaning *(Thank You Lord) in the Malawian language known as *Chichewa*.

By, Atupele F Mwaungulu

Acknowledgements
My Lord and Savior
Family, Friends, Mentors and Acquaintances

CHAPTERS

1. Creation
2. Darkness
3. Dwelling Place
4. Every day is a New Day
5. God is watching
6. God's Kingdom
7. Grace
8. He is My True Peace
9. Hour after hour
10. I Remember You
11. It is a Beautiful Day
12. I've (I Have)
13. Keep on Praying
14. Lost and Found
15. Love never fails
16. Lovely
17. Miracles
18. My Heart's Desire
19. New Days
20. Samaritan Journey
21. Waking Up
22. We all Need God
23. We've got to come together
24. You got to have faith

Reference
About Author/ Back Cover

*"Spread love everywhere you go.
Let no one come to you without leaving happier."*

Quote by Mother Teresa

Creation

Who gave us life that we can breathe?
We want to go out and seek new opportunities.

Who gave us sunshine so bright and clear?
We want it to stay all day and near.

Who gave us the moon to glow at night?
As we walk our paths we fear no sight.

Who made the mountains so great and tall?
The valley's and streams flow endlessly below.

Who made the birds to soar in the clouds?
They seem to sing a song to God.

Darkness

I have lived as a prodigal

I have had a time of fun in the mix of the party

I have danced under the sun until I got tired

Then I came to my senses

And I knew best to lay all my shame at God's altar

Why I am still locked up in darkness

I need to be free from this sin formed within the darkness

God knew I was still learning in this faith walk

I would still stumble and fall in all kind of allies

Season by season I seemed to be growing wiser

Again I came to my senses

And I knew best to lay all my sorrow at God's altar.

Why I am still locked up in darkness

I want to be free from this sin formed within the darkness.

Dwelling Place

Walking down the road today was all I could do
As I listened for your quiet voice to tell me what to do
I was going through the usual trials that make me walk from you
So I prayed that moment and I felt so good.

I am thankful Lord that I can come into your loving grace
And I can learn to worship you in spirit and in truth.
What would I do without your love you gave?
I would be somewhere in the wilderness without your loving ~~hand~~ grace.

Every day is a New Day

Every day is a new day!
Don't you think you deserve it?

Every day is a new day!
See how wonderfully you are made.

Every day is a new day!
Don't give up on life yet.

Every day is a new day!
Because you are ready to love!

Every day is a new day
Don't forget that.

God is watching

God is watching

Lights blinking

Cars are creeping

Night full of dancing

Central Parks dreaming

Camera's flashing

Subway's moving

God is watching

Loves Romancing

News is saddening

Beggars singing

Lights never sleeping

Planes are soaring

Bikers whistling

God is watching

And the Statute of Liberty is a-standing

Gods' Kingdom

There is a time in our life when we shall see God's kingdom.

A New Heaven and a New Earth

It shall be a place called paradise with angelic beings flying

The crystal river a – splashing and tree of life a-lighting

In an instance a soul shall change and meet the great I-AM they say

You will have your own room with your name on it!

Walking and talking, possibly meditating and praying?

What about crying and singing?

With kids a-playing to animals howling?

I don't really know, but I can on and on reflecting on this new

Heaven and New Earth a-coming

Grace

Grace came down from heaven like raindrops and filled my cup.

I was longing and waiting for that heavenly grace just like that.

I never knew of such a heavenly feeling from above.

As I was sitting alone in the distant cold land,

I cried like a new born baby when suddenly I felt raindrops fill my cup.

Oh, grace came down from heaven like raindrops and filled my cup.

But to each one of us grace was given according to the measure of Christ's gift.
Ephesian Chapter 4: verse 7

He is My True Peace

In this life I make sure the path I take is his light and the journey is definitely not easy.

I am reminded of the prodigal son who returned to his father quite uneasy.

As I move forward in this life myself the enemy always tries to block me.

I have to get down on my knees and pray for my soul's protection.

With my eyes closed and my heart ready I pray.

I have to trust and lean on God my everlasting,

As I pray I feel a thunder of demons fleeing,

Good doors open and bad doors close;

And I begin to feel this peace surround me.

Then I slowly open my eyes and look around and begin to believe in this true peace.

Hour after Hour*

In this world of expectation one learns to lean on many things you name one
Hour after Hour
What happens when all expectations all fall short like right now
We murmur but cannot quickly overcome.
Hour after Hour
Trusting and asking God for answers.
Some are answered and most are not!
Hour after Hour

So what to do
What to say
Humble our hearts and pray?
Love not fight
Eat home goods
Drive with ease
Try and sleep with ease
Wear different masks
Sing the Birthday song with the water flow
Hour after Hour

As most families sit by home windows trying to be safe;
The kid's minds are itchy to feel that wind,
Sun and rain outside the window pane
Hour after Hour

wrote this poem during the Covid-19 year of 2020

where it affected many homes and my own health

I Remember You

I give you both praise and honor

You walked upon a path given to you.

I look at what you raised and I will never forget your words of wisdom and love.

I remember you.

Mother is what you are to me.

Father is what you are to me.

I know we will meet in eternity and oh what joy it will be.

I remember you.

It is a Beautiful Day

It is a beautiful day because God is in this place

It is a beautiful day because God's love is everywhere

It is a beautiful day as trees and flowers are blossoming

Lying by the flower bed as butterflies flutter across my mind

I remember Momma telling me to be cautious of this heart.

I understand now what she was saying as I feel the hot sun beam heating me up.

It is still a beautiful day because life is in the air

It is still a beautiful day because joy is everywhere

It is still a beautiful day as I daydream by this flower bed.

……thinking of Momma who loved flowers

I'VE (I Have)

I've wanted to go back to my worldly ways and God waits on back.
I've sinned again and again and landed on my face and God lovingly holds me back.
I've broken down my door to have my way and God always puts it back.
I've cried and cried until my eyes got so crimson wide and God always has my back.

I've laughed like Sarah, wept like Hannah and God blessed me back.
I've walked tirelessly to the well in the heat of day and God had my back.
I've lain on my bedroom floor waiting for the Lord to break through and he has had my back.
I've had moments at God's feet and He has been silent towards this back.

Author's Words

Greetings,

Poetry Corner is a collection of short poems I wrote to encourage myself in the faith. I hope you are inspired by them.

Zikomo Ambuye*
Meaning *(Thank You Lord) in the Malawian language known as *Chichewa*.

By, Atupele F Mwaungulu

Acknowledgements
My Lord and Savior
Family, Friends, Mentors and Acquaintances

CHAPTERS

1. Creation
2. Darkness
3. Dwelling Place
4. Every day is a New Day
5. God is watching
6. God's Kingdom
7. Grace
8. He is My True Peace
9. Hour after hour
10. I Remember You
11. It is a Beautiful Day
12. I've (I Have)
13. Keep on Praying
14. Lost and Found
15. Love never fails
16. Lovely
17. Miracles
18. My Heart's Desire
19. New Days
20. Samaritan Journey
21. Waking Up
22. We all Need God
23. We've got to come together
24. You got to have faith

Reference
About Author/ Back Cover

*"Spread love everywhere you go.
Let no one come to you without leaving happier."*

Quote by Mother Teresa

Creation

Who gave us life that we can breathe?
We want to go out and seek new opportunities.

Who gave us sunshine so bright and clear?
We want it to stay all day and near.

Who gave us the moon to glow at night?
As we walk our paths we fear no sight.

Who made the mountains so great and tall?
The valley's and streams flow endlessly below.

Who made the birds to soar in the clouds?
They seem to sing a song to God.

Darkness

I have lived as a prodigal
I have had a time of fun in the mix of the party
I have danced under the sun until I got tired
Then I came to my senses
And I knew best to lay all my shame at God's altar
Why I am still locked up in darkness
I need to be free from this sin formed within the darkness

God knew I was still learning in this faith walk
I would still stumble and fall in all kind of allies
Season by season I seemed to be growing wiser
Again I came to my senses
And I knew best to lay all my sorrow at God's altar.
Why I am still locked up in darkness
I want to be free from this sin formed within the darkness.

Dwelling Place

Walking down the road today was all I could do
As I listened for your quiet voice to tell me what to do
I was going through the usual trials that make me walk from you
So I prayed that moment and I felt so good.

I am thankful Lord that I can come into your loving grace
And I can learn to worship you in spirit and in truth.
What would I do without your love you gave?
I would be somewhere in the wilderness without your loving ~~hand~~ grace.

Every day is a New Day

Every day is a new day!
Don't you think you deserve it?

Every day is a new day!
See how wonderfully you are made.

Every day is a new day!
Don't give up on life yet.

Every day is a new day!
Because you are ready to love!

Every day is a new day
Don't forget that.

God is watching

God is watching

Lights blinking

Cars are creeping

Night full of dancing

Central Parks dreaming

Camera's flashing

Subway's moving

God is watching

Loves Romancing

News is saddening

Beggars singing

Lights never sleeping

Planes are soaring

Bikers whistling

God is watching

And the Statute of Liberty is a-standing

Gods' Kingdom

There is a time in our life when we shall see God's kingdom.

A New Heaven and a New Earth

It shall be a place called paradise with angelic beings flying

The crystal river a – splashing and tree of life a-lighting

In an instance a soul shall change and meet the great I-AM they say

You will have your own room with your name on it!

Walking and talking, possibly meditating and praying?

What about crying and singing?

With kids a-playing to animals howling?

I don't really know, but I can on and on reflecting on this new

Heaven and New Earth a-coming

Grace

Grace came down from heaven like raindrops and filled my cup.
I was longing and waiting for that heavenly grace just like that.
I never knew of such a heavenly feeling from above.

As I was sitting alone in the distant cold land,
I cried like a new born baby when suddenly I felt raindrops fill my cup.
Oh, grace came down from heaven like raindrops and filled my cup.

But to each one of us grace was given according to the measure of Christ's gift.
Ephesian Chapter 4: verse 7

He is My True Peace

In this life I make sure the path I take is his light and the journey is definitely not easy.
I am reminded of the prodigal son who returned to his father quite uneasy.
As I move forward in this life myself the enemy always tries to block me.
I have to get down on my knees and pray for my soul's protection.
With my eyes closed and my heart ready I pray.
I have to trust and lean on God my everlasting,
As I pray I feel a thunder of demons fleeing,
Good doors open and bad doors close;
And I begin to feel this peace surround me.
Then I slowly open my eyes and look around and begin to believe in this true peace.

Hour after Hour*

In this world of expectation one learns to lean on many things you name one
Hour after Hour
What happens when all expectations all fall short like right now
We murmur but cannot quickly overcome.
Hour after Hour
Trusting and asking God for answers.
Some are answered and most are not!
Hour after Hour

So what to do
What to say
Humble our hearts and pray?
Love not fight
Eat home goods
Drive with ease
Try and sleep with ease
Wear different masks
Sing the Birthday song with the water flow
Hour after Hour

As most families sit by home windows trying to be safe;
The kid's minds are itchy to feel that wind,
Sun and rain outside the window pane
Hour after Hour

wrote this poem during the Covid-19 year of 2020
where it affected many homes and my own health

I Remember You

I give you both praise and honor

You walked upon a path given to you.

I look at what you raised and I will never forget your words of wisdom and love.

I remember you.

Mother is what you are to me.

Father is what you are to me.

I know we will meet in eternity and oh what joy it will be.

I remember you.

It is a Beautiful Day

It is a beautiful day because God is in this place
It is a beautiful day because God's love is everywhere
It is a beautiful day as trees and flowers are blossoming

Lying by the flower bed as butterflies flutter across my mind
I remember Momma telling me to be cautious of this heart.
I understand now what she was saying as I feel the hot sun beam heating me up.

It is still a beautiful day because life is in the air
It is still a beautiful day because joy is everywhere
It is still a beautiful day as I daydream by this flower bed.

……thinking of Momma who loved flowers

I'VE (I Have)

I've wanted to go back to my worldly ways and God waits on back.
I've sinned again and again and landed on my face and God lovingly holds me back.
I've broken down my door to have my way and God always puts it back.
I've cried and cried until my eyes got so crimson wide and God always has my back.

I've laughed like Sarah, wept like Hannah and God blessed me back.
I've walked tirelessly to the well in the heat of day and God had my back.
I've lain on my bedroom floor waiting for the Lord to break through and he has had my back.
I've had moments at God's feet and He has been silent towards this back.

Keep on Praying

There is a God out here who can love you He is everything you need
He has all the things you ask and you will receive.
Such as prayer for comfort and prayer for loving!
There is a love out in the world that is so untender and it leaves one in a state of gloom!
It is not what God offers your life hardly blooms.
You may get rough edges or a pathway that leaves you blind

What does one have to do to be on such a path?
What does one have to do?
Keep on praying?
What does one have to do?
Learn to keep up with the universe?
What does one have to do?
Read an inspirational message?
What does one have to do?
Trust in God.

Lost and Found

As I sit alone in my room a still small voice echoes through my mind.

I try to hide all by myself but this small voice still calls.

When I start to doze in the dark room my ears still hear the voice.

I begin to peddle with the emotions of church bells ringing to people laughing.

Day by day

Night by Night I am so weary.

I wonder should die right here or go back home.

Or just leap up like a baby gazelle and go back home.

But why do I still hear that still small voice call?

Love Never Fails

There was a time I was searching for my own love in many books of my own
And every moment that I captured I would be all alone
I made it so complicated until I gave up my search.
You see love is created by God from above.
I know I have to be patient and let God put us as one.
So blessed is the man who finds the woman he loves.
Yes blessed is the woman who finds the man she loves.
Love Never Fails.

Lovely

My life has been easy living here at home
I have had moments when I had nowhere to go
Even through the seasons when it was so dark
Jesus you were able to give me your love.

I am thankful you are the answer to every hardship in life
Without you here I wonder what each day would be like
I am so grateful I can enter into your loving grace.
And worship in your lovely sanctuary all day long.

Miracles

Do you believe in miracles that happened in the Bible?
Do you believe in miracles that God created the universe?
Do you believe in miracles of the Israelites?
Do you believe in miracles where Jesus turned the fish and the bread to feed the hungry ones?
Do you believe in miracles that God sent his son Jesus on the bloody cross?
Do you believe in miracles that God is watching us from heaven gates?
Do you believe in miracles that you get saved?
Do you believe in miracles today?

My Heart's Desire

As I sit in the heart of the circle with friends I see what my heart desires.

As I sit in the church pews and gaze up ahead I see what my heart desires.

As I walk silently through the crowd I smile at those around and see what my heart desires.

As I talk with those I know so well, you silently appear and stand in my midst I see what my heart desires.

As I go for a walk along the grassy plains, I sit and gaze at the beauty and see what my heart desires.

As peace envelopes my mind I embrace the force of nature and know what my heart desires.

New Days

New days are good for dancing

New days loving hands are holding

New days are filed with people laughing

New days are good for playing

New days children are praying

New days are when the sun is shining

New days are when birds are singing

New days are busy with people working

New days are good.

Samaritan Journey
(Luke 10:30-35)

There was a man who was travelling down a weary road when some thieves saw him coming, and robbed him of his clothes.

The thieves left him dying to care for his soul when two men came passing, but never looked upon.

Then another man with his donkey stopped beside this dying man.

He shook his head with great sorrow, and took him to a place where he would be cared for in peace.

You too may find yourself on the Samaritan road, maybe your neighbor or friend needs your help.

So take a moment to reach out and give them a hand.

Waking Up

Waking up in the Morning I am to seek your face.
Knowing it would help me throughout the day.
Without you hear beside me what do I say?
There are times I wake up all ashamed
I don't know how to praise you when I wake.
I get so frustrated some days.
I look at myself in the bathroom mirror glance and walk away,
Then I slowly begin to open the dark curtains so you can enter in.
And you tell me that you love me in such a special way.

We All Need God

In a world of confusion many souls are lost on rocky roads.

Our only refuge and hope is Jesus Christ our Lord.

And the peace that flows from heaven heals broken souls.

We all need peace, love and God.

In a world of confusion there is still hope

Never give up when there is so much to hold

Yes never give up on the walk called hope.

We all need peace, love and God.

Regardless of your circumstances one needs to lean on God.

We've got to come together

We've got to come together

Sisters and Brothers of many colors

We've got to come together

Just as God taught us

Never turning backwards but moving on forward.

We need not be so judgmental

But loving on one another

We need to help each other

Just as God taught us

Never turning backwards but moving on forward

Come along everybody

Come along everybody.

Come along let us walk together.

You got to have faith
You got to have faith
You got to have faith in the Lord
You got to believe
You got to believe in the Lord

You got to have faith all the time
You got to be wise in your mind
You got to be all right
You got to have faith

The Lord told us to believe
You just tell the mountain to be cast into the sea and you will be free
So you got to have faith.

Reference
The Holy Bible, New Living Translation (NLT)

Made in the USA
Middletown, DE
11 October 2022

Keep on Praying

There is a God out here who can love you He is everything you need
He has all the things you ask and you will receive.
Such as prayer for comfort and prayer for loving!
There is a love out in the world that is so untender and it leaves one in a state of gloom!
It is not what God offers your life hardly blooms.
You may get rough edges or a pathway that leaves you blind

What does one have to do to be on such a path?
What does one have to do?
Keep on praying?
What does one have to do?
Learn to keep up with the universe?
What does one have to do?
Read an inspirational message?
What does one have to do?
Trust in God.

Lost and Found

As I sit alone in my room a still small voice echoes through my mind.

I try to hide all by myself but this small voice still calls.

When I start to doze in the dark room my ears still hear the voice.

I begin to peddle with the emotions of church bells ringing to people laughing

Day by day

Night by Night I am so weary.

I wonder should die right here or go back home.

Or just leap up like a baby gazelle and go back home.

But why do I still hear that still small voice call?

Love Never Fails

There was a time I was searching for my own love in many books of my own

And every moment that I captured I would be all alone

I made it so complicated until I gave up my search.

You see love is created by God from above.

I know I have to be patient and let God put us as one.

So blessed is the man who finds the woman he loves.

Yes blessed is the woman who finds the man she loves.

Love Never Fails.

Lovely

My life has been easy living here at home
I have had moments when I had nowhere to go
Even through the seasons when it was so dark
Jesus you were able to give me your love.

I am thankful you are the answer to every hardship in life
Without you here I wonder what each day would be like
I am so grateful I can enter into your loving grace.
And worship in your lovely sanctuary all day long.

Miracles

Do you believe in miracles that happened in the Bible?
Do you believe in miracles that God created the universe?
Do you believe in miracles of the Israelites?
Do you believe in miracles where Jesus turned the fish and the bread to feed the hungry ones?
Do you believe in miracles that God sent his son Jesus on the bloody cross?
Do you believe in miracles that God is watching us from heaven gates?
Do you believe in miracles that you get saved?
Do you believe in miracles today?

My Heart's Desire

As I sit in the heart of the circle with friends I see what my heart desires.

As I sit in the church pews and gaze up ahead I see what my heart desires.

As I walk silently through the crowd I smile at those around and see what my heart desires.

As I talk with those I know so well, you silently appear and stand in my midst I see what my heart desires.

As I go for a walk along the grassy plains, I sit and gaze at the beauty and see what my heart desires.

As peace envelopes my mind I embrace the force of nature and know what my heart desires.

New Days

New days are good for dancing

New days loving hands are holding

New days are filed with people laughing

New days are good for playing

New days children are praying

New days are when the sun is shining

New days are when birds are singing

New days are busy with people working

New days are good.

Samaritan Journey
(Luke 10:30-35)

There was a man who was travelling down a weary road when some thieves saw him coming and robbed him of his clothes.

The thieves left him dying to care for his soul when two men came passing, but never looked upon.

Then another man with his donkey stopped beside this dying man.

He shook his head with great sorrow, and took him to a place where he would be cared for in peace.

You too may find yourself on the Samaritan road, maybe your neighbor or friend needs your help.

So take a moment to reach out and give them a hand.

Waking Up

Waking up in the Morning I am to seek your face.
Knowing it would help me throughout the day.
Without you hear beside me what do I say?
There are times I wake up all ashamed
I don't know how to praise you when I wake.
I get so frustrated some days.
I look at myself in the bathroom mirror glance and walk away,
Then I slowly begin to open the dark curtains so you can enter in.
And you tell me that you love me in such a special way.

We All Need God

In a world of confusion many souls are lost on rocky roads.
Our only refuge and hope is Jesus Christ our Lord.
And the peace that flows from heaven heals broken souls.
We all need peace, love and God.

In a world of confusion there is still hope
Never give up when there is so much to hold
Yes never give up on the walk called hope.
We all need peace, love and God.

Regardless of your circumstances one needs to lean on God.

We've got to come together
We've got to come together
Sisters and Brothers of many colors
We've got to come together
Just as God taught us
Never turning backwards but moving on forward.

We need not be so judgmental
But loving on one another
We need to help each other
Just as God taught us
Never turning backwards but moving on forward

Come along everybody
Come along everybody.
Come along let us walk together.

You got to have faith
You got to have faith
You got to have faith in the Lord
You got to believe
You got to believe in the Lord

You got to have faith all the time
You got to be wise in your mind
You got to be all right
You got to have faith

The Lord told us to believe
You just tell the mountain to be cast into the sea and you will be free
So you got to have faith.

Reference
The Holy Bible, New Living Translation (NLT)

Made in the USA
Middletown, DE
11 October 2022